Affirming the Ph.D. Within

Motivation to Walk the Journey to the Phinishline

JESSYE L. B. TALLEY, Ph.D.

For Publishing Information, contact Journal Joy at Info@thejournaljoy.com.

www.thejournaljoy.com

———————

Paperback ISBN: 978-1-957751-78-8

Hardback ISBN: 978-1-957751-50-4

Editor: Oju Ajagbe & Nicole Gyimah

———————

Second paperback edition, 2024

TABLE OF CONTENTS

DEDICATION

This book is dedicated to every aspiring and future Doctor of   Philosophy (Ph.D.). Remember: "To whom much is given, much is required." Learn as much as you can, enjoy the process, and keep in mind — it's all about endurance. See you on the other side!

You've got this,

Dr. Jessye L. B. Talley

ACKNOWLEDGEMENTS

First, I want to acknowledge God for His insights that have brought the pages of this book to life. To my husband and son, for being my constant motivators throughout this process. I want to thank my parents, who always push me to do things with a spirit of excellence.

- To my sister, who traveled this doctoral journey at the same time as myself.

- Dr. Lauren Davis, my Advisor, who pushed me beyond my limits and helped me to see my full potential as a scholar and researcher.

- To every participant of Sisters Scholars, you drive my work to see an increase in the number of African American/Black Ph.D. holders in all areas of Science, Technology, Engineering, and Mathematics (S.T.E.M.) and beyond— you helped me write this book.

- To Stephen Jarrelle Harris of Relnice Photography— thank you for my book cover photos; these are my favorite images of myself at graduation.

- To Tiffany Lewis, for helping me focus and stay committed to the writing process.

- To Oju Ajagbe, your keen eyes plus copy editing and proofreading skills helped refine my words.

I am thankful for all of you and the roles you played in bringing this book to life. Thank you!

INTRODUCTION

Hello, I'm Dr. Jessye L.B. Talley and I almost didn't complete my Doctor of Philosophy (Ph.D.) degree. I know — that sounds like a horrible first line to begin this book, but it's true. The fact that I almost gave up on attaining my Ph.D. is the very reason why this book is now in your hands. This book was birthed straight out of my Ph.D., experience. Are you feeling challenged on your journey? If yes, I can certainly empathize and sympathize with you at this very moment. What I desire to share with you in the pages that follow are some of the lessons I have learned and things I wish I could have done a little differently throughout my Ph.D. journey.

You may be wondering how this book's title, *Affirming the Ph.D. Within: Motivation to Walk the Journey to the Phinishline*, came to be. The first reason, I love reciting affirmations — I understand the power of affirming myself daily. The second motivator stems from my Ph.D. completion journey. There were many times that I was down or discouraged and did not want to complete this degree. Sometimes, I did not always have motivating factors to push me on. Or, at crucial moments I would not be able to reach a specific person that I urgently needed/wanted to talk with, either on the phone or via a videoconference platform. So, may this book be a source of great encouragement — especially during those times when you feel like you do not have what it takes and/or the tools you need to keep on going.

I did not always enjoy the process — and many people hinted along the way that I was, "doing too much." (That was their code phrase for saying, "Jessye you are stressing yourself out; you need to pause and take breaks.") Some days, I wish I had simply listened because I never took a break. I basically went straight through in terms of completing my three academic degrees back-to-back: Bachelors, Masters, and

Ph.D. There were many days that I asked myself, "Jessye — why did you do this to yourself?"

Did you pick up this book because you are continuously asking yourself the question, "Why am I even pursuing this Ph.D. degree?" People have various reasons and answers to that question. At the end of the day, if you are determined to attain your Ph.D. then that response should be solidified. I believe that as you go through the pages of this book, you will be affirmed in your decision, and know that a Ph.D. degree doesn't define you — nor your unique journey to completion. If you have decided to go this route, then you are already a Doctor of Philosophy (Ph.D.).

What I like to tell people is that once you have made up your mind to attain a Ph.D., you are now just going through the process to make it official. In the chapters that follow, I will share insights about different aspects of my Ph.D. journey— from discovering my "Why" to successfully making it across the Phinshline.

I'm believing that as you go through the pages of this book, you will glean new insights and strategies, be encouraged to happily continue on your Ph.D. journey, and joyfully get hooded at your graduation ceremony. Use this book as your support when no one is available to take your call; when you're up alone trying to get through writing or completing experiments; and— especially when you're ready to throw in the towel.

Now, let's get started and *Affirm the Ph.D. Within*. Let's get to it, Doctor— the world needs your giftings! Before we begin, I want you to fill out the next page: **"TARGETS."**

Targets

Dr. _____

Discipline: _____

Proposal Date: _____

Defense Date: _____

Graduation Date: _____

B.P. (Before Ph.D.)

"I NEVER LOSE. EITHER I WIN OR LEARN."

— NELSON MANDELA[1]

---

[1]Master Academia. December 21, 2022. Top 10 Motivational quotes for Ph.D. Students. Retrieved from https://master-academia.com/phd-motivational-quotes/.

CHAPTER 1
So, You Want To Get A Ph.D.?

You would not believe how many students come up to me and ask the following questions:

"Why should I pursue a Ph.D.?"

"What are the benefits of pursuing a Ph.D.?"

I then always hit them with this question: ***Do you really want to get a Ph.D., or have you made this decision because of someone else?***

At this point, those students are either looking at me like I'm crazy or are visibly baffled because they don't know how to answer my question. The truth is, the Ph.D. process is not necessarily an easy one and you must ***devote lots of time*** to it; therefore, it's very important that you make your decision wisely. What I mean is: you need to make this choice based on ***your*** specific life goals and plans. Once again, I'm asking you— YES, ***you*** who's reading these words —"So, you want to get a Ph.D.?" If you answered "Yes," then that's great — I'm excited that you have decided to go on this journey! Now, I will begin to share *my* story and the process that got me to this point.

My Ph.D. journey began all the way back in 2008, which was my senior year of undergraduate studies. I had applied and interviewed for several jobs; however, nothing seemed to be going through. So, I decided to apply for graduate school. I like to think of this decision as "Divine Intervention." Remember: When something is not working out quite right, then something else, much better, is just around the corner. I chose to apply to graduate school because I had previously been in a program established by my parents called "Joint Educational Facilities (J.E.F.)." This program sparked my interest in conducting research, writing ten-page papers, and presenting at conferences— while I was still in high school. I decided that I wanted to keep on going to school and see if I would be accepted. I was accepted and began the journey of obtaining my Master's degree.

I started off with pursuing my Master's degree in Industrial and Systems Engineering. During this degree journey, I was able to work with students more and I continued to develop my skills in the area of operations research. When I got close to graduation, I was back in the same dilemma. Should I apply and interview for jobs or should I apply for the Ph.D. program? I actually did ***both*** again! To be transparent, part of my choice to do both was two-fold— due to familial expectations and because of my desire to make an impact on future generations. I realized that to get to my final decision, I needed to ask myself three (3) questions that would give me insight and solidify my answers.

1. "Why do I want to pursue a Ph.D.?"

2. "What do I hope to achieve?"

3. "What steps will get me there?"

So, why did I pursue my Ph.D.? Like I mentioned earlier, partly because of familial expectations— my Dad has a Ph.D. in Business Administration. Secondly, the first career I ever wanted to pursue was teaching. I love helping students, really all people, learn and better understand various topics. I also love to work on research that is focused on providing innovative solutions to societal problems. Ultimately, the biggest reason why I decided to pursue my Ph.D. degree was because I wanted to be a successful example for students that look like me— especially African American/Black female students. I have been fortunate enough to have had teachers at almost every education level that looked like me. Sadly, many students still do not. So, I wanted to do my part in helping to start changing that narrative. I also wanted to be in a position to act as a trusted resource to help ensure greater success for students at every education level.

My desire is to impact many future generations of engineers. To assist in successfully producing more African American/Black Ph.D. holders in various disciplines— because they chose to stay the course and complete their degrees. To see more African American/Black students, in general, pursue research opportunities and graduate school degrees in the areas of Science, Technology, Engineering, and Mathematics (S.T.E.M.).

To get to this point, I needed to stay connected to a good mentor, have a strong support system, and pursue a variety of opportunities to prepare me for this new journey ahead. I also needed to create a good, strategic plan. We will discuss all of these topics in later chapters.

The funny thing about this three-question assessment is that you will need to continue referring back to it throughout your Ph.D. journey. These three questions will help to keep you grounded— and also help you to get back on track when you fall off. They will remind you of your reason(s) for pursuing this degree, or as I like to call it— your "Why." Your "Why" will help push you ***through*** to your Phinishline.

Now that you understand your "Why," completing the application process should be much easier. So, let's talk about the application process and package.

A competitive Ph.D. application package will consist of a Statement of Purpose, Letters of Recommendation, Transcripts, and the actual Application. Let me break down the first two elements: Statement of Purpose and Letters of Recommendation.

Statement of Purpose

Your Statement of Purpose needs to give the application reviewers a clear sense of the following things:

1. Who are you?

2. Why are you pursuing this degree?

3. Why are you pursuing this degree ***now***?

4. Why did you choose ***this*** department and university, specifically?

In addition to making sure that you fully address these four questions, you can enhance your Statement of Purpose by doing your homework in order to possibly "name drop." Make sure to thoroughly review the faculty members who have similar research interests and reach out to them. Why is this helpful? They may have some funding already available— and they can advocate for you during their department's deliberation time. At least one (1) sentence regarding this should go into your Statement of Purpose. Another thing to include: two to three (2–3) sentences stating why you chose to apply to this specific school and program. Ultimately, you should stick to two (2) pages, maximum, for your Statement of Purpose.

Letters of Recommendation

Seek out multiple people to write ***supportive*** Letters of Recommendation for you. I would say three (3) people is good, as that is normally the number of letters that you need to submit. It is helpful to also send copies of your Resume and Statement of Purpose, so the different people writing your Letters of Recommendation have information outside of what they already know about you to glean from. You should always choose people that can speak to your strengths and skills. Anything you would like them to highlight should also be in your Resume and Statement of Purpose.

Bonus Insight: Funding

After determining the degree program(s) you will apply to, it is important to check out the funding available. Most schools have specific scholarships or fellowships for their graduate school students and possibly for your specific discipline. You can also see what is available through the professional organization(s) connected to your discipline.

Another way to consider funding is to check out the lab websites for the faculty members that have similar research interests as you. You can reach out and/or fill out their application(s) to inquire about research or teaching assistantships. Please note that you will not always receive a response right away. I also recommend that you share how your interests align with the lab and what you hope to gain from the experience.

In conclusion, I want you to consider your answers to those three questions. Just like me, you will discover "Why" you should pursue this degree and the benefits. Really dig deep as you ponder because this is a life-changing experience. Now, let's put into practice affirming yourself before we leave this chapter.

My "Why" gives me clarity about my future.

I have found a Ph.D. program that fits my "Why" and it's paid in full.

I am successfully making an impact in my chosen industry and/or profession.

NOTES, THOUGHTS, and REFLECTIONS

"YOU DON'T GO AS FAR AS YOUR DREAM. YOU GO AS FAR AS YOUR TEAM."

— DR. DHARIUS DANIELS[2]

2Nieuwhof, Carey. "CNLP 356: Dharius Daniels on Leading with Relational Intelligence, Leadership Learned the Hard Way, and the Keys to Great Communication." July 20, 2020. The Carey Nieuwhof Leadership Podcast. Published by Carey Nieuwhof. Podcast. Audio. 1 hour 14 minutes. https://careynieuwhof.com/episode356/.

CHAPTER 2
Building Your Ph.D. Team

Congratulations are in order if you have made it past Chapter 1! It is safe to say that you have put in some applications and are either waiting to hear back or you have been accepted into the program(s) of your choosing. Even if you have not heard anything (*yet*), it does not mean that you cannot build your Ph.D. support team.

So, let's pause.

If you are like me, then you like to give names to the people or things that are special to you. Now, before you continue with the rest of this chapter, I'm leaving space for you to come up with a name for your Ph.D. support team. Your team will consist of all the people associated with helping you to make it across your Phinishline. I've listed a couple of examples, below, to get your wheels turning.

1. Network

2. Starting Lineup

3. Squad

4. Posse

5. Board of Directors

6. Group

7. Core Team

Write your Ph.D. support team's name here:

_____

This is exciting! You have a name for your Ph.D. support team; now, you must decide whom you would like to navigate this journey with you. This decision is _crucial_ to your success! There are three (3) very important types of people that you need on your team (and in your greater network). They are: Mentors, Advocates, and Sponsors.

A **_Mentor_** can be defined as a person who's a trusted counselor, guide, or teacher.

An **_Advocate_** is a person who supports and promotes a cause or group.

A **_Sponsor_** is a person who vouches or is responsible for a person or thing.

Contrary to popular belief, all of these roles do not need to be found in the same person. So, with these roles in mind, I want you to think about the top five (5) people who must be in your core group— the "VIPs" of your Ph.D. support team. These are your behind-the-scenes people. They are the ones in the trenches with you… These are the people you can truly call at any moment— they will pick you back up, especially when you want to quit. List their names, here:

1. _____

2. _____

3. _____

4. _____

5. _____

Now that you have established your core group (within your Ph.D. support team), I want you to write down your top overall needs, at this moment, in the following four (4) categories: Spiritual, Professional, Mental/Emotional, and Leisure/Recreation. Once you have listed out your current needs in each category, I want you to create subcategories because you may have multiple needs. Then, list all of the people that fall within these four (4) categories— including those already in your core group and Ph.D. support team. Lastly, I want you to go back and fully review all the people you have listed; make a note by each name as to what role(s) they should fulfill throughout your Ph.D. journey— whether as a "Mentor (M)," "Advocate (A)," or "Sponsor (S)." This will help you determine the best people to reach out to when you have a specific problem and/or question.

Spiritual
Current Needs:
Subcategories:
People:

Professional
Current Needs:
Subcategories:
People:

Mental/Emotional

Current Needs:
Subcategories:
People:
Leisure/Recreation
Current Needs:
Subcategories:
People:

These four (4) categories may now include some new people that you would like to join your Ph.D. support team. Let's talk about some ways to approach introducing yourself and asking these people you don't already know to be a part of your Ph.D. journey and support team.

1. Send out cold e-mails and/or LinkedIn requests, explaining why you want to connect.

2. Connect after a research talk at a conference.

3. Follow up after securing an introduction through a trusted mutual connection.

4. Organically strike up a conversation.

Below, write down your plan(s) for reaching out to the new people you've listed in these four (4) categories.

_____

_____

_____

_____

_____

_____

_____

_____

_____

_____

_____

_____

_____

_____

_____

_____

Dissertation Key Players

Additionally, your Advisor(s) and Dissertation Committee members are also part of your greater Ph.D. support team. Your Advisor(s) and Dissertation Committee members are the key players that will help you to navigate your Dissertation process smoothly.

Advisors

I like to call Advisors the "gatekeepers" because in the end they must sign off and approve all of your submitted work. They will give the approval for you to prepare for— and pass— your Dissertation Proposal and Defense stages. They also help to develop the researcher in you. As you can see, their support is crucial for these very important tasks and milestones while on your Ph.D. journey.

Dissertation Committee Members

When your Advisor(s) is (are) not readily available, your Dissertation Committee members should step in to help you. It is crucial that you pick the right people. Sometimes, you might have to navigate the various layers of office politics that exist within your chosen discipline(s)/field(s) of expertise's department(s).

If your next question is, "How do I select an Advisor (or Advisors) plus Dissertation Committee members and develop these relationships?" please keep reading!

When determining who to select as your Advisor(s) and Dissertation Committee members, keep in mind the following:

1. Pick people who align with your values— this is vital.

2. Pick people with whom you can share your difficulties as well as your triumphs.

3. Pick people who will not only motivate you, but also point you in the right direction— plus provide you with various resources.

4. Pick people who are willing to give you timely, honest, direct, and constructive feedback.

5. Pick people who will readily share opportunities for your continued professional development.

6. Pick people who value you maintaining wellness in all areas of your life.

7. Pick people who clearly align with your chosen discipline(s)/field(s) of expertise.

Additionally, you must make sure that your Advisor(s) and Dissertation Committee members can all work together. Them being able to get along with each other and *__focus on your success__* will help your Dissertation process to run a little more smoothly. You also want to make sure each person has a background in some methodology you will be using, so that you can ask focused questions as needed. You want people who will *__not__* hold you up—or cause any unnecessary problems. After ensuring that your choices for your Advisor(s) and Dissertation Committee members all satisfy these criteria, email each person and do a formal ask.

One thing to remember with your key players is that being an Advisor or a Dissertation Committee member is not their only role or professional position. It is important to do what you can to make things easier for them to give you timely, honest, direct, and constructive feedback when needed. Setting up a consistent weekly meeting schedule with your Advisor(s) and Dissertation Committee members is key to keeping them aware of where you are in your Dissertation process.

Scheduling weekly meetings was key in helping me to get the feedback I needed to keep progressing. I tried to post the information I wanted to review in our shared space at least a day or two before our meeting each week. That way, my Advisor could easily get up to speed quickly. These kinds of proactive measures are especially helpful if your Advisor(s) and Dissertation Committee members have a large research team.

Dissertation Coach

Now, this key player gets a lot of flak within the Ph.D. community. A lot of people will say this is a scam and a waste of money— since you already have your Advisor(s). Indeed, your advisor(s) is (are) supposed to provide assistance; however this is not always the experience for everyone. Let me share why I added a Dissertation Coach to my Ph.D. journey.

In the fall of 2014, I decided to reach out to a Dissertation Coach because I felt like I was not making as much progress as I desired or had anticipated. The expectations in front of me were frustrating— and I was beginning to feel like I could not make it to my Phinishline.

So, I reached out to a Dissertation Coach and we set up a weekly time to connect. From that time onward, we would meet every Tuesday at 4:00pm. This time slot was perfect because it was right before I had my weekly meeting with my Advisor. At times, my Coach literally felt like one of my Dissertation Committee members. She was the sounding board who looked over everything I planned to submit before I discussed it with my Advisor.

As a result of working with my Coach, my weekly Advisor meeting times were better utilized. I was getting better feedback and I progressed onto my Dissertation Proposal by the next semester. Also, my Proposal was so well put together, thanks to all of my Coach's guidance, that my Dissertation Committee members had no questions— and were very impressed.

So, if you need that extra support then I encourage you to reach out to a Dissertation Coach. At times, **_you need to invest in your success_**. I was glad I did; my Dissertation Coach literally provided me with the extra accountability I needed in order to move forward and progress quickly.

The key reason for me enlisting the aid of a Dissertation Coach— and the word that consistently keeps me going, even now— is **_accountability_**. Accountability pushes me to sit and get things done. Accountability helps me to not settle. Accountability connects me with like minded peers that also want to excel. Accountability helps me to trust myself and my actual abilities. Accountability leads me to connect with people who see my potential. Accountability also leads me to help others. Without accountability, I would not have my Ph.D. today.

I encourage you to choose wisely. Make sure the people in your Ph.D. support team, your core group (the "VIPs"), and your ever-expanding network will all truly want to hold you accountable— especially when _**you**_ need it the most.

Congratulations on developing your Ph.D. support team (plus coming up with a team name), establishing your core group (the "VIPs"), selecting your Advisor(s), as well as Dissertation Committee members (maybe even adding a Dissertation Coach), and consistently expanding your Ph.D. network!

Before we leave this chapter, I want you to remember a couple of things. Mentorship and my network have been vital keys to my success. I also make sure to give room for these relationships to change over time, based on each individual's personal growth and Divine revelation. Now, let's affirm this great support network you are developing.

I can find the right people— who can also provide me with resources that will help me excel.

I am walking with support for every area of my life.

Accountability helps me to thrive.

I am cultivating my ground to receive value.

I am open to new connections that take me outside of my comfort zone.

"ACTION IS THE FOUNDATIONAL KEY TO ALL SUCCESS."

— PABLO PICASSO[3]

3Master Academia. December 21, 2022. Top 10 Motivational quotes for Ph.D. Students. Retrieved from https://master-academia.com/phd-motivational-quotes/.

CHAPTER 3

Where Are Your Plans?

As you embark on your Ph.D. journey, you need to have a High-level Dissertation Plan and a couple of Detailed Dissertation Plans. What do I mean? Your High-level Dissertation Plan maps out your overall doctoral process from beginning to end. Your Detailed Dissertation Plans focus on specific areas within your High-level Dissertation Plan that you need to map out further.

Let's talk about why you need to create these plans— and why you need to do this action ***at the beginning*** of your Ph.D. journey.

1. These plans help you gain back time. During your Ph.D. journey, time is very crucial and goes by extremely fast.

2. These plans help you and your Advisor(s) stay on the same page about where you are in the process.

3. These plans hold you accountable. If you send your plans to someone else (in addition to your Advisor(s) and Dissertation Committee members), then you'll have double the accountability.

4. These plans help you work more efficiently because you know exactly what to focus on at specific times.

So, let's talk about creating your High-level Dissertation Plan and then your Detailed Dissertation Plans.

High-Level Dissertation Plan

Your High-level Dissertation Plan should not be super detailed; still, it should include all the major milestones associated with completing your Ph.D. degree. To start, you can use Microsoft Excel or Word and then later transfer the working file into a productivity management program, such as Asana, Trello, or another one preferred/used by your fellow peers/cohort or graduate school.

You can begin crafting your High-level Dissertation Plan by creating a table like this:

Proposed Semester	Actual & Estimated Time	Task	Deadline Status	Adjustments	Note

Using this table format, write out the Semester(s) you plan to complete specific (milestone) "Tasks." Examples of Tasks include: the writing of chapters, data collection, creating presentations for your Dissertation Proposal and Defense, etc. Then, write down the actual Estimated Date(s) and Time(s) you will work on each Task. I encourage you to put down actual dates and times because they will come to mind more readily—especially when you know you have work to do with a deadline attached. If you are not sure, you can put a specific length of time (e.g., "2 weeks" or "2 months"). You should also enter these dates and times into your calendar(s) to ensure successful scheduling.

The "Deadline Status" column is very similar to crossing something off a list; however, you are putting the status of your work (i.e., "Completed," "[Still] In Progress," "Not Started," "Pending Review," etc.). The "Adjustments" column comes into play when you have circumstances that delay your work and/or progress on these listed Tasks. So, you will just write down the new date and/or time for your revised deadlines. After your weekly meetings with your Advisor(s) (or Dissertation Committee members or Dissertation Coach) and/or after completing a Task, you should write down all the Notes associated with the entry in order to keep up with important points, as well as track your progress made in stages/phases for specific Tasks.

Again, you want to make your High-level Dissertation Plan tasks pretty broad to help keep you on track and know where you are headed over the next couple of years. You can also add more columns if needed.

At a minimum—I advise you to review and update your High-level Dissertation Plan _**after**_ each semester, so that the most accurate information is consistently being shared with your Advisor(s), Dissertation Committee members (plus Dissertation Coach), core group (your "VIPs"), and others in your greater Ph.D. support network. After completing your High-level Dissertation Plan, you can start developing your Detailed Dissertation Plans for specific tasks.

Detailed Dissertation Plans

Your Detailed Dissertation Plans should breakdown the big tasks that will take a month or longer to complete. This can also be helpful when it's time to create outlines for your writing. Let's use the following example from my Ph.D. journey to illustrate this point.

During year three of my doctoral program, I began to map out the steps I needed to take to complete my Dissertation Proposal. A big part of this process was to have the written form of my Proposal completed. Looking at all the required parts of a Dissertation Proposal was daunting; however, the key to my successful planning was breaking down this big (milestone) task into smaller chunks.

Here is an example of the table I created to help me break down my Dissertation Proposal task into smaller chunks. My "Major Tasks" were the titles for each chapter I needed to complete for my Dissertation Proposal. The "Subtasks" were related to the second-level headings included under each chapter. The "Sub-subtasks" were the third-level headings and a shorthand outline of what I would discuss under the second-level headings. This same process can be used to create your Dissertation Presentation as well.

Major Tasks	Subtasks	Sub-subtasks

These detailed plans are great for coming up with how you will schedule your time blocks devoted to writing your Dissertation and conducting your research. Now, we will delve into these two areas: your writing and research plans.

Writing Plan

Your writing plan should be somewhat similar to the table I created to help me break down my Dissertation Proposal (milestone) task into smaller chunks. Your plan should break down your Dissertation Proposal into chapters, so you can schedule focused chapter-writing time blocks. Again, this is your mechanism for ***accountability***. You want to be as detailed as you can in your outline and have a structure to your writing process.

Please also keep in mind that finding citations, researching other information, formatting, making revisions, etc. are also considered part of your writing process. Lastly, whatever you do, work on developing a consistent practice. Use note-taking applications to always stay in writing mode. Mark where you stopped writing, so you know where to start in the future. When you have completed your Dissertation Proposal draft, it might be beneficial to hire a Dissertation-focused copy editor and proofreader to correct your spelling, punctuation, and grammatical errors, plus review and revise your formatting— making sure it is done correctly throughout your document before you officially submit your Proposal to your Advisor(s).

Two Dissertation Structures

Structure 1: Traditional

The Traditional structure is typically used when writing your Dissertation. Your Dissertation will include these sections: Introduction, Literature Review, Methodology, Results, Discussion, and Conclusion. I used this structure format when I wrote my Master's thesis, since I hyper-focused on one main topic. There are other sections you can add that are more specific to your chosen discipline(s)/field(s) of expertise's area(s) of research. Your graduate school's website should have a handbook (or guidebook) that shows you the approved format(s) for your specific institution. They also should have a session each semester to go over guidelines and deadlines for when your Ph.D. document(s) should be submitted.

Structure 2: Convert to Journal Articles

The Convert to Journal Articles structure is used when you want to easily convert sections of your Dissertation into a publication-ready journal article format. This was the structure I used for my Ph.D. Dissertation, since I developed multiple models. I had a main Introduction that highlighted the motivation for my Research and gave a high-level snapshot of my challenges plus the contents of my Dissertation. Each chapter after that was based on a model I developed. My chapters were written and formatted following the Traditional structure. This meant that each chapter could easily be taken and submitted to academic publications.

As you are writing your Dissertation, pick the best structure that will cut your time in half when you need to submit it to publications. Most institutions have this as a requirement before you graduate.

Research Plan

If you are like me, you had specific methodologies that you were using to develop your research; it is imperative that you map out this process. You need to set aside ample time to learn how to best utilize the technology and/or resources you have available to aid/support your research. Next, you need to determine your research structure.

Research Structure

This structure could be the number of times you work on your research, when you run experiments, analyzing your data, etc. This is crucial to making significant progress on the meat of your Dissertation. If your modeling is not done, then writing becomes difficult. At the end of the day, words on paper get you closer and closer to your Phinishline!

After creating all of these plans (your High-level Dissertation Plan, Detailed Dissertation Plans, Writing Plan, and Research Plan), it is important to then share them with your Advisor(s), Dissertation Committee members (plus Dissertation Coach), and core group (your "VIPs"). Your Advisor(s) and Dissertation Committee members (plus Dissertation Coach) can then share their insights and other steps you might need to take in order to make it across your Phinishline. Sharing these plans with your core group will also provide a safe space for you— as well as the always-needed accountability. This way, everyone is on the same page—plus can ensure all your plans are clear and attainable.

Along with these plans, you should set up a daily schedule. A daily schedule will help you to enter each task into your designated time slots—ensuring everything is in alignment. In your daily schedule, incorporate down time because you must make sure your body has the chance to rest and reset— in preparation for what is still to come.

Each semester, I created a master block schedule to successfully incorporate down time, daily.

Time	Monday	Tuesday	Wednesday	Thursday	Friday	Saturday	Sunday
8-9am	Preparation	Preparation	Preparation	Preparation	Preparation		
						Preparation/ Breakfast	Preparation/ Breakfast
9-10am	Leave for campus	Leave for camp	Leave for camp	Leave for camp	Leave for campus	Breakfast	Breakfast
10-11am	INEN 430	Office Hours	INEN 430	Dissertation	INEN 430	Dissertation	
					Meet with Committee Member		
11-11:30	Prepare for meeting						
11:30-12:30pm	Meet with Advisor						
12:30-1pm	Lunch						
11-12noon		Office Hours	Office Hours	Dissertation		Dissertation	Church
12-1pm		Lunch	Lunch	Lunch	Lunch	Lunch	Church
1-2pm	Office Hours				Dissertation	Dissertation	Dissertation
2-3pm	Dissertation	Dissertation		Dissertation	Dissertation	Dissertation	Dissertation

Updates

As you continue your Ph.D. journey—and begin to see how you're progressing through your plans, it's important to communicate your milestones. One of the biggest resources that I implemented during my Ph.D. process was generating a weekly update.

What you may not know is the level of assignments already stacked on your Advisor's (or Advisors') and Dissertation Committee members' plates. On top of that, if they have multiple students, it is very easy to fall through the cracks— and you could end up still working on your research a year or two later.

Since we met weekly, I would submit my (Dissertation Coach-reviewed) written synopsis regarding what I was working on before our scheduled appointment. This helped my Advisor and Dissertation Committee members to better see that I was making progress— and being intentional about working through my problem areas.

Two things occurred as a result of me implementing this proactive strategy. Firstly, my meetings were better regarding the quality feedback I received. Secondly, I could track my milestones better throughout my doctoral journey.

Here is the format I used for my weekly meetings:

Individual Meeting – [Insert Date]

List what I accomplished during the week.

List any problem areas or questions with the current project.

List next steps.

The key takeaways from this chapter are: communicating your goals effectively, putting your plans in place, and establishing your accountability. These three strategies will lead to a successful doctoral process for you. Today, take the time to start creating all your plans. Before we leave this chapter, let's affirm these great plans you're now developing and refining.

I am committed to my Ph.D. journey.

I create successful and attainable plans.

I am accountable to myself and others.

I will make it across the Phinishline.

"IF YOU DON'T WRITE, NOTHING WILL CHANGE."

— UNKNOWN[4]

4Master Academia. December 21, 2022. Top 10 Motivational quotes for Ph.D. Students. Retrieved from https://master-academia.com/phd-motivational-quotes/.

CHAPTER 4
On the Road to Candidacy

Once your classes are complete, you will spend time taking exams you must successfully pass in order to then become a "Ph.D. Candidate." The process you go through can vary slightly, depending on your chosen discipline(s)/field(s) of expertise and institution. I will share my process and some strategies plus tips that you might find helpful.

My department had two different tests: a Qualifying Exam and a Preliminary Exam. I first took the Qualifying Exam and was then required to take an individual test focused on the core areas of my Ph.D. discipline; both results were then tallied to determine my final score. I had to get a specific combined final score in order to pass the Qualifying Exam step. Thankfully, both the Exam and test were open notes style.

For me, a challenging aspect of this Exam was its duration —from like 8:00am to either 3:00pm or 4:00pm (pretty much a full workday) with a lunch break.

Here are some strategies plus tips for taking the Qualifying Exam.

1. Start your studying the **<u>semester</u>** **_<u>before</u>_** you take the Exam—preferably at the same time as your cohort. I had about six to seven (6–7) topics to study. I made sure I had a clear plan for each topic. My cohort and I were each given a binder and could go to all the professors that created the Exam to inquire about the specific topics that would be covered.

2. The week before— make sure you have all the resources and notes you need for each topic organized so you can easily find information during the Exam.

3. The night before— make sure to get as much rest as possible; do your best to go to sleep early.

4. The morning of Exam Day— eat a good breakfast, pack lots of snacks and a hearty lunch — you will need the energy.

5. During the Exam, **read through all the questions _first_** to see which ones you can accurately answer without needing to search through your notes.

6. Pace yourself during the Exam. When it's time to take a break, utilize it well to give your brain a pause.

7. After completing your Exam, double and triple check your answers before turning it in.

These strategies plus tips served me well on my Exam Day. However, in full transparency, my results showed that I did not get the required combined final score needed in order for me to pass the Qualifying Exam step. I was devastated. The silver lining—I was allowed to retake one of my lowest-scoring sections. I studied everything involving that topic and consulted with the professor who created the make-up exam. The results after my retake showed I got enough points to pass! The first hurdle was complete.

The second exam I took was the Preliminary Exam, which consisted of individual exams administered by each of my Dissertation Committee members. And I had six (6) people on my Committee… I know, I know—what was I thinking?! Thankfully, they were all very supportive of my work and what I was doing. My six (6) exams were given all at one time and based on my Dissertation Committee members' area(s) of expertise. I was given just one (1) week to complete all of them. That was one of the longest weeks of my life.

If you ever question why you got yourself into your Ph.D. program, this would be the time. It almost seemed like they intentionally picked questions that were completely mind-boggling. But these exams were crafted to challenge me!

Before I share more about my experience, here are some strategies plus tips for taking the Preliminary Exam.

1. During the fixed length of time you are given to complete your Preliminary Exam step, do not answer any phone calls, do not waste time leisurely going out with your family/friends, nor entertain any other forms/types of distractions. You need to stay super focused.

2. Plan your meals, schedule your sleep times, and insert small pauses to just let your mind rest. If you do not make room for breaks, you will burn out and waste valuable time. I was fortunate enough to have someone from my church kindly prepare a couple of meals that lasted me the entire week. All I had to do was heat them up. Now, you can use DoorDash, UberEATS, and more—utilize these food delivery services. Remember that you also need sleep. I slept in predetermined intervals because every minute was precious.

3. When you receive all of your tests, spend an hour or two just reading through them to see where you want to start first. Then, map out a plan for how you will tackle each question. This will save you time in the long run because you know where you need to focus your energy.

Don't lose hope when discouragement sets in—especially if the solution is not coming. Take a small break and work on another question; eventually, the solution will come to you.

4. Make sure to save all your work where you can quickly access it—and do so in multiple places.

5. After you have successfully completed the Preliminary Exam step, take a couple of days for lots of fun and downtime, so you can get back to work on your research rejuvenated and refreshed.

Upon completion of my Preliminary Exam, I found out I had passed… but needed to do some things over. Now, in my mind, I did not pass— if I still had to make revisions. I went to each of my Dissertation Committee members and asked what I needed to do to fully pass their respective exams. I made those corrections and then I received the great news that I could officially call myself a "**Ph.D. Candidate!**" I was so, so happy! Now, it was time for me to focus on writing my Dissertation Proposal.

During this time, affirmations and encouragement are very important because you may have more down moments than usual. Here are a few affirmations that will help you throughout this part of your Ph.D. journey.

I have the resources to help me be successful and pass all of my exams.

I am a successful Ph.D. Candidate.

My mind, body, and spirit deserve rest.

I am equipped with timely solutions.

"BELIEVE YOU CAN AND YOU'RE HALFWAY THERE."

— THEODORE ROOSEVELT[5]

5Master Academia. December 21, 2022. Top 10 Motivational quotes for Ph.D. Students. Retrieved from https://master-academia.com/phd-motivational-quotes/.

CHAPTER 5
Emotional Rollercoaster

We often hear about the emotional rollercoaster of going on the Ph.D. journey. It also takes a toll on our mindset. You may have heard from lots of people that the doctoral process is more about endurance. This is very true— you must make sure to get your mindset right in order to persevere. Some common mental barriers Ph.D. Candidates often deal with are needing external validation, overcoming times of failure, resisting imposter syndrome, managing perfectionism, and even (sometimes) working through an identity crisis.

Each one of these mental barriers can also be deeply rooted in past trauma experienced way before the Ph.D. journey began. No matter where you are currently in the process, I implore you to find a *counselor and/or therapist. For some experiences or situations, we may need external help to process and/or overcome them.* You will become a better you!

Now, let's explore each one of these mental barriers and some possible steps you can take to encourage forward momentum in a positive way. We will end this chapter with how you can create a Self-care Plan. As you read through this book, I desire for you to learn and implement strategies that will encourage you throughout your Ph.D. journey and help you to cross your Phinishline as a healthy, whole person.

Needing External Validation

Now that I am a Professor, it would not be right for me to start off without defining what we are talking about here. Validation is defined as the act or process of making something valid, ratifying it, or checking that it satisfies certain standards or conditions (Oxford Reference, 2023).

Now, I want you to sit with that for a moment. Then, I want you to answer these two (2) questions: "How does the definition of *validation* inform what I think about myself and my Ph.D. journey at this moment? What does this mean?" Let's process these questions.

Throughout the doctoral process, we seek validation from our peers, Advisors, Dissertation Chairs, and Dissertation Committee members. Going back to the definition, what are we **really** doing? Yes, we need feedback on our Ph.D. work and are working with top experts in their respective fields. However, what are we oftentimes subconsciously saying to ourselves? We are saying to ourselves that we constantly need someone else to validate (acknowledge) what we are doing. This, in turn, can lead to codependency—constantly feeling stuck unless another person gives their approval to take action. We should not take what we have to offer only at face value, thus decreasing its value— and ultimately resulting in us losing sight of what we can **authentically** bring to the table.

The subconscious need for continuous external validation can leave us in a place of doubt and constantly questioning our intelligence. Do you see how a person can quickly spiral out of control due to these thoughts during their Ph.D. journey? Attaining a Ph.D. is already hard enough; no need to add more to the process. Then how do we continue to validate ourselves when it gets tough? We focus on knowing our *worth*.

Worth

Worth is defined as the value of something measured by its qualities or by the esteem in which it is held (Merriam-Webster, 2023). Wait a minute—this sounds a lot like the definition I shared for *validation*.

So, how does someone else know **_your_** *worth* or value? Right now, I want you to go to a mirror, look at yourself, and ask yourself this question out loud. "So, how do others know **_my_** worth or value?" Yes, ask yourself this question right now. I am sure it hits different seeing your face and internalizing it. What answer did you discover?

In my opinion, the answer is that others cannot tell me what to think of myself because they don't know me; however, they can influence how I view myself. Only after observing me can they try to either enhance or damage my personal feelings about my worth and/or value.

Take for instance my son, who is very young. He is still learning how to communicate and navigate through life in the world. When he grows up and leaves home, others will try to influence him in various ways that will not always be good. As his mother, I have the responsibility to guide him through the world and show him how to cultivate plus maintain a healthy sense of self-worth and value. Therefore, no matter what anyone says about your work or your "unconventional" Ph.D. journey, you must choose to hold yourself in high esteem. You must internally know the value of what **_you_** bring to the table. This is how you can overcome needing the external validation of others.

Overcoming Times of Failure

Failure may show up often throughout our Ph.D. journey. Sometimes, it can seem like a never-ending process. It happens so frequently that we become numb and entertain quitting almost every day. Failure can be synonymous with performance. It's a blatant attack on our self-worth. It has a way of making us shrink back. It gets us to a place where we do not pursue. We basically put a lid on our potential— and progress. We believe these **limits** should remain intact. **Limits** only box us in, stifling our creative thinking, and resulting in us underperforming. We no longer want to take risks; we sit in complacency— and become stagnant. These are just some of the negative side effects due to embracing failure. Failure is not all bad— it simply depends on our perspective.

Winning

I love listening to songs with uplifting lyrics that are all about **winning**! That's really what we want to do—___win all day___, ___every day___! However, did you know that failing and making mistakes can also be seen as ___wins___? I know, it doesn't feel like it. Still, let's go there for a minute.

Remember that small tester experiment you did that happened to mess up? Well, you actually then found out that one of your parameters was wrong— thankfully ___before___ you wasted tons of money, precious materials, and valuable time. Your "mistake" actually saved you lots of heartache. Your Dissertation Chair sent you major edits and suggested implementing a different approach to your research design. Well, you then realized that this new approach is perfect; everything you need to do is now in seamless alignment versus the process you had been struggling with before receiving your Chair's extensive feedback. Both of these instances can initially seem like really bad occurrences; however, they were actually small miracles in disguise.

One word to describe winning is ___success___. How do you define success? What does success look like— for you? How do you know when you have reached it? It might not be what you expect. You must take every little thing you accomplish as a win and use your wins to propel you forward.

Take out at least one (1) blank sheet of paper and write down everything you have accomplished on your Ph.D. journey so far. When you are done, I want you to put that piece (or those pieces) of paper on display. A bonus would be to frame it (them) because your accomplishments are amazing. Let this piece (or these pieces) of paper and all the accomplishments you listed remind you that you are out here killing it—especially when things get tough.

Resisting Imposter Syndrome

We hear this term a lot. Some people hate it, and some people identify with it very well. If it resonates with you, then that means at some point you have felt like a fraud. You felt like somebody was going to figure out that you have just been pretending to know what to do in this role all along. It's synonymous with acting— convincingly portraying someone else so well, while wearing a mask.

That's tough! It's not fun walking around most of the time feeling like you are not at a certain level, when in all reality you truly are doing the dang thing. Fight against lowering the bar that you've set for yourself because of how your circumstances and other people are making you feel. How do you overcome imposter syndrome? It will take intentionality and lots of reminders. It's you tapping into who you really are— not focusing on what others think/say about you. Through various life experiences, we have created so many narratives about ourselves that it takes a moment to see through these façades.

Authenticity/Truth

Authenticity is so important because it helps you see through any façade. I define *authenticity* as who you are at your core— without the influence of any outside force. It's when you show up and don't have to change anything about yourself to please others. It's when you feel comfortable bringing your whole self to the table.

You might be thinking, "Dr. Talley, this sounds great and I hear you. *How do I* ***choose*** ***authenticity***?" Let's start by pondering on a few statements and questions.

1. Write down on a typical day the types of messages you are telling yourself.

2. Write down on a typical day the types of messages others are telling you.

In each instance, I want you to think about the emotions or feelings that are tied to these messages. Before we move on, I want you to sit with this for a moment and really dig deep. These messages (plus the emotions or feelings they trigger), whether you realize it or not, drive you to move and act in certain ways. Some of those ways can sadly be very detrimental.

Now that we have some awareness, let's try to process through the emotions or the feelings that are not beneficial to our success or forward movement. I want you to think back to when you first encountered these emotions or feelings; those moments in time were when negative experiences were planted into your memory. These were the foundational moments where you accepted beliefs that were not true and internalized them deep into your subconscious. So, we need to process through them and see what we can learn. Again, take a moment to sit with these new insights.

Now that we know where these false beliefs came from, it's time to develop new core values and beliefs to replace the lies preventing our true authenticity from showing.

Let's go through an example.

Lisa is in the third year of her Ph.D. journey. She is finishing up her coursework, and has a handle on her Dissertation topic in order to get started with her research. This semester, she is really having trouble while other students seem to be moving forward. She starts to entertain doubt and begins to tell herself, "I cannot do this… I should not even be here." Every time she sits down to do her work, she cannot figure out why it takes so much effort to get anything done— or why she feels out of place while sitting in her classes.

Since she was tired of feeling this way, Lisa chose to do something about it. She paused and reflected on the very first moment she felt like this. She remembered a class where she tried to answer questions only to get the answers wrong. She also remembered the questions she received during one of her class presentations that really made her feel like she didn't measure up to where she needed to be in her Ph.D. program. At that moment, Lisa decides that a change of mindset is needed. What she wants to focus on feeling is **_confidence_**. She then wrote out this statement:

"I am well equipped with knowledge/resources— I deserve to be in this program. I have what it takes to succeed."

After placing this reminder in visible areas throughout her home and workspaces, it was easy for Lisa to stop and recite these life-affirming words— helping her to get back on track faster in those tough moments.

May going through this exercise have the same impact for you and bring you to the place of always being authentically yourself, everywhere.

Managing Perfectionism

Perfectionism is defined as the standard, attitude, or philosophy that demands perfection and rejects anything less (Dictionary.com, 2023). I like to define it as the never-ending standard we give ourselves to attain. Perfectionism always leaves you feeling as if you are striving for something that you can't quite grasp. When you do make it, you barely notice because you're already thinking about the next thing. The truth is we will never be perfect; yet, we can aim to always do our absolute best!

I love this quote by Dr. Brené Brown from her book *Dare to Lead: Brave Work. Tough Conversations. Whole Hearts.*: **"Perfection is not the same thing as striving for excellence. Perfection is not about healthy achievement and growth. Perfection is other focused!"** (Brown, 2018).

When I first read these words, they really hit me— all the way to my core. They reminded me of how perfection puts us outside of where we want to be. Perfection has us creating expectations that were not meant for us. Perfectionism does not promote growth; it keeps us in this endless cycle of needing external validation and never hitting the bullseye. The standard always seems just out of reach. Perfectionism constantly keeps our focus on the future… and can enable chronic procrastination. One way to manage perfectionism is with mindfulness.

Being Present in the Moment (Mindfulness)

Have you found it difficult to just focus on the current day? Do you find yourself moving back and forth between tasks? When you finally lay down to sleep, is your mind still racing? If you answered "yes" to some or all of these questions that means you are staying in a place of worry. When you expend your energy worrying, your mind is not at peace and it's quite hard to stay/be present in the moment.

Right now, I want you to pause reading this book and close your eyes; imagine what staying/being present in the moment would look like for you. Set a timer for five (5) minutes and just process through this. When the timer goes off, I want you to take some time to journal about this experience. How do you feel? Does it seem almost insurmountable to stay/be present in the moment?

I will admit it can be very hard for me, especially since I have more of a Type A personality— I don't readily take the time to celebrate my small wins. I just move on to the next task, which only brings me back to that perpetual state of perfectionism I don't desire. Once I was introduced to some mindfulness principles, two stuck out to me and I want to share them with you (Kabat-Zinn, 2013).

1. Judgment

2. Beginner's Mind

Whether we realize it or don't, we judge ourselves and others often. Our judgments come as a result of perceived deficiencies, lack, and comparison. Judgment keeps us in the mindset of "should've," "could've," "would've." Focusing on hypothetical scenarios does not help us to stay/be present in the moment.

Remember—once time is gone, we cannot get it back. The time we have left _**can**_ be redeemed, if we use the proper perspective. We should also practice going into different situations with a "Beginner's Mind." This means we should try to not let our previous knowledge hinder us from being open to receiving/learning new knowledge.

Being open gives us a wider perspective about embracing multiple options for how scenarios/decisions can pan out.

Working Through an Identity Crisis

During your Ph.D. journey, it is easy to have an identity crisis. An *identity crisis* is defined as a developmental event that involves a person questioning their sense of self or place in the world (Dowler, 2022). The world of Academia, oftentimes an environment full of questions, doubting, and loneliness, is fertile ground for experiencing identity crises.

Identity crises push us further away from who we are at our core. It leaves us open, if we are not careful, to the lies we have heard about ourselves through other people. At moments like this, when you are super struggling, I want you to go back and re-read Chapter 1. Ask yourself the three (3) questions:

1. "Why do I want to pursue a Ph.D.?"

2. "What do I hope to achieve?"

3. "What steps will get me there?"

The funny thing about this three-question assessment is that you will need to continue referring back to it throughout your Ph.D. journey. These three questions will help to keep you grounded— and also help you to get back on track when you fall off. They will remind you of your reason(s) for pursuing this degree, or as I like to call it—your "Why." Your "Why" will help push you ***through*** your Phinishline. Reread your previously written answers to these three questions and revise/add to them, if needed.

Utilizing the positive strategies found in every chapter of this book serves as a form of identity theft protection. We are internally monitoring what is going into our minds— ensuring that we are valuing and nurturing the correct narratives about ourselves.

What Is Your Identity?

To combat having an identity crisis, we need to be solidified in our identity. Think about this for a minute. What makes you... **_you_**? What is your make up? These are the unique characteristics that control how you see the world. They block out all the criticism and negative words that have been spoken about and over you. They help you to rise to the occasion and produce. They remind you that *you're only in competition with yourself*. Therefore, remember who you are and where you come from, so you can get to where you are going!

Now that we have discussed each one of these mental barriers, we can begin to develop a Self-care Plan.

I want to preface this Plan by saying that "self-care" has become a buzzword—what some people might call "self-care" may not fully align with the term's true essence. Self-care allows you to take inventory of where you are physically, emotionally, mentally, and spiritually. All those areas should be cared for differently.

Self-care plans will look different for each person; still, they should include these following components:

Physically

- Create an exercise regimen.

- Get your yearly physical exam.

- Take your vitamins.

- Follow your meal plan.

- Take care of your appearance.

- Get regular massages.

Emotionally/Mentally

- Consider getting a counselor/therapist.

- Journal regularly.

- Have a core support group you can check in with often.

- Listen to a motivational podcast.

- Go on retreats.

Spiritually

- Spend time in prayer.

- Meditate regularly.

- Connect with like-minded believers.

- Listen to uplifting music.

- Listen to sermons/teachings.

- Fast periodically.

As we close out this chapter, I hope that you have gained a new appreciation for who you are and how your story impacts your research and overall Ph.D. journey. I also hope you feel better equipped to combat negative thoughts when they arise. Make sure to *follow* your Self-care plan. Now, let's take the time to affirm what is going right, despite the highs and lows of this emotional rollercoaster journey.

I value and honor who I am during this process.

I prioritize myself during this process.

I am present and can stay in the moment.

I know who I am; I show up authentically as myself.

I am physically, emotionally, mentally, and spiritually strong.

"IF YOU GET TIRED, LEARN TO REST, NOT TO QUIT."

—UNKNOWN[6]

6Master Academia. December 21, 2022. Top 10 Motivational quotes for Ph.D. Students Retrieved from https://master-academia.com/phd-motivational-quotes/.

CHAPTER 6
Relationships

As you progress through your doctoral process, it's important that you take the time to intentionally cultivate relationships that will help you move forward. Earlier, in Chapter 2, we talked about creating your core group (the "VIPs") within your Ph.D. support team and greater network. Now, we are going to discuss assessing and maintaining your platonic and/or romantic relationships as you complete your Ph.D. degree. Here is some insight into my romantic relationship journey.

I met my husband in 2005 while we were completing our undergraduate degrees. Since we were both Engineering majors, it was somewhat easy to spend a lot of time getting to know each other. Upon graduation, we both decided to pursue our Master's degrees— once again in Engineering and at the same university. As we continued our relationship, we learned more about each other's lives and long-term goals. Based on the challenges and triumphs we experienced during those years, we learned how we each coped in certain environments and in particular situations.

After completing our Master's degrees, in 2011, my boyfriend (now my husband) went to Seminary— and I started my Ph.D. journey. Our continued education put us in different states for the first time— our relationship was now long-distance.

We talked every day. We tried to meet up for the holidays. For some breaks, I went to visit him to give myself time away from my Ph.D. work. Even before we were physically apart, we knew our relationship stance and how we felt about each other. Thankfully, our long-distance season made us a stronger couple.

My boyfriend (now my husband) graduated from Seminary a few years before I would officially complete my Ph.D. journey and cross over my Phinishline. So, In

2015, we were physically back together— now to prepare for our wedding day. During our wedding season, I took a break from my Dissertation work.

Upon our return home from our honeymoon, I began to learn how to balance my work and home life. It was important that I took the time to develop a schedule that clearly divided my time between work, family, and rest.

In the last year of my doctoral journey, my husband began an internship in a different state and I soon followed him. In my final months, he needed to leave the country; as he was leaving, he said, "I will be calling you 'Dr. (Mrs.) Talley' [when I return]; so, get it done."

After passing my Defense (and eating a celebratory lunch), I began my drive home— arriving just as my husband was being dropped off from the airport. When I told him I was ***Phinished***, he said, "I knew it all along." His unwavering support was everything.

I encourage you to choose your life partner wisely. As you can now see, your Ph.D. journey requires time away from your loved ones and you will miss some special family events/moments/traditions. Your doctoral journey requires you to work and do ***a lot***. You need a lot of encouragement along the way. Be careful— it is very easy for your family, partner, friends, colleagues, etc. to get jealous and feel neglected if they're coming along on this journey with you. Be sure to plan moments where they can have some of your undivided time and attention. Be sure to stick to your boundaries—and work on improving your communication skills.

Communication is key. It might be helpful to invite your family and/or partner into your doctoral process. There were many times my husband read through my in-progress Dissertation document and gave me invaluable feedback.

What you will also discover is that even certain friends and friendships may come and go. Until you establish your (solid) core group, your Ph.D. journey can seem quite lonely. Since you have a limited time schedule, you will need people to be flexible. Unfortunately, not everyone will understand that their access to you needs to change (even if temporarily). And, it might be difficult to really explain to others what you are doing or working on. It is ok. Oftentimes a lot of Ph.D. students find an understanding community among their cohorts. The main key is communication— and learning how to connect with the right people in ways that will not overwhelm you.

I will end this chapter by saying that **anybody** can start off being supportive, but can also quickly become jealous, a distraction, disagreeable, and a source of negativity plus discouragement during your Ph.D. journey. Such people should be left at a distance once you notice their behavior shift. The mental and emotional capacity you need to focus on your doctoral process should not be wasted on relationships that will hinder you.

Whoever joins you on this journey should only add encouraging momentum to your successful crossing of your Phinishline. Your Ph.D. graduation is a major celebration for you as well as those who supported you— especially the relationships closest to you. Now, let's affirm your ability to better manage your evolving platonic and/or romantic relationships.

I deserve platonic and/or romantic relationships of value.

I am connecting with people that help me fulfill my purpose.

I am open to receiving help from Divine connections.

I am the type of friend to others that I want in my life.

"YOU ALONE ARE ENOUGH. YOU HAVE NOTHING TO PROVE TO ANYBODY."

— MAYA ANGELOU[7]

7Master Academia. December 21, 2022. Top 10 Motivational quotes for Ph.D. Students. Retrieved from https://master-academia.com/phd-motivational-quotes/.

CHAPTER 7

I Am Finally a Doctor of Phiosophy (Ph.D.), Well, This Is Anticlimatic!"

<hr>

During the months leading up to my Dissertation Defense, I diligently worked day and night to complete my Ph.D. degree. At this point, I was so over this journey—I just wanted to be done. I spent countless hours working on my required revisions plus getting my Dissertation Defense Presentation together.

Remember: this was all happening during my first year of marriage—and we'd just moved to a new state, Richmond, VA- meaning I was now *hours away* from Greensboro, NC, my graduate school's campus! I spent a lot of time in my car driving between these two states; it was very draining.

A few days before my Dissertation Defense Day, I drove down to my school to prepare. As I sat down with my Advisor, I felt like I was making great progress. Then, I got hit with some major revisions. I'm not going to lie, I left our meeting feeling like the work I had done these past couple of years was completely changed… that I might not know what I was talking about. I was really in a state of worry and defeat. It was not as smooth sailing compared with when I completed my Dissertation Proposal. I stayed up for a while fixing what I could in time for my Defense Day (the next day), and was still able to sleep for a couple of hours.

I woke up tired and a bit nervous about the day ahead. I was finally at Defense Day; I should have been happy. In reality, it was one of the longest, most draining days of my life. I got my Dissertation Defense Presentation set up and waited for everyone to join me in our conference room.

While I waited, I saw one of my peers; he gave me a word of advice I'd like to also share with you. He told me, "Jessye, don't stress—you are the expert about your work. Just walk in there confidently." Another person also advised me not to stress—I needed to just focus on doing what I came to do: successfully defend my work and leave with my Ph.D. degree.

I also had a good showing of supporters, which I definitely needed. While I only spoke for an hour, it seemed like *forever*. I was getting tired of talking and really hoped I was making sense, due to all the revisions I'd just made overnight. When I reached the last slide and said, "This concludes my presentation. Are there any questions?" I was so happy and felt the biggest release. I could breathe again.

My Dissertation Committee members asked me a couple of questions; then, it was time for me and my supporters to leave the room so they could begin their Deliberation. Their Deliberation time also felt like it went on for forever plus a day! At last, my Advisor came out smiling and said, "Congratulations, **_Dr._** Talley." All of my Dissertation Committee members said the same greeting and gave me some final words. Then, we all ate lunch together in the conference room.

Honestly, I did not know what I was expecting/supposed to feel. I do know that right after I finished, the waiting during Deliberation was very anticlimactic for me. I asked my peers and my Advisor, "Is this really what it's supposed to feel like? I'm done; yet, I don't have an over-the-top happiness feeling."

I was a little crushed by my lack of enthusiasm because it was supposed to be so much more. After eating lunch, and once I started driving off campus, it really hit me that I was now a **_Doctor of Philosophy (Ph.D.)_**. A weight had literally been lifted from my shoulders. What I'd worked so hard for was truly complete. I spent the rest of my Defense Day getting acclimated back into society; more about this in the next chapter. Now that I have shared how I crossed my Phinishline, let's talk about some strategies and tips to help you prepare for your Dissertation Defense Presentation.

At last, you have received the approval from your Advisor(s) that you can reach out to your Dissertation Committee members to schedule your Final Defense. Let me tell you, those are the best words to hear— you're truly nearing the very end of your doctoral journey! So, where do you begin?

1. **Department Guidelines**

Each institution is different. Find out if your school has a specific length of time requirement in between submitting your Dissertation Proposal and scheduling your Dissertation Defense. Make sure you are following those guidelines. Also, make sure you know the timeline for when to send your final Dissertation document to your Dissertation Committee members. Usually, your final Dissertation document should be submitted about two (2) weeks *before* your Final Defense.

2. **Document Preparation**

At this point, your Advisor(s) has (have) read through your Dissertation document and given you ample feedback in order to truly finalize your Dissertation. Make sure you utilize the guidelines and documentation standards required by your graduate school/institution. When scheduling your Final Defense, do so after you have sent your final Dissertation document to your Committee members— so they have time to read through it before Defense Day.

3. **Presentation Preparation**

In general, you have roughly one (1) hour to present a culmination of all the work you have done for your Ph.D. degree. Start off with a basic outline of the high-level points from your Dissertation document. Make sure your presentation tells an easy-to-follow story with diagrams and/or visuals, if possible, instead of multiple slides full of text.

Remember, back in Chapter 3 we discussed the two structures you can use to write your Dissertation document. You can also use these two structures to outline your Dissertation Defense Presentation with the following formats. Each of these main sections can be broken down further.

The Two Dissertation Structures

Structure 1: Traditional

- Title Slide

- Agenda

- Introduction

- Literature Review

- Methodology

- Results

- Discussion

- Conclusion

- Future Work

- References

- Questions

Structure 2: Convert to Journal Articles

- Title Slide

- Agenda

- Introduction

- Literature Review

- Methodology

- Model 1 or Area 1

- Model 2 or Area 2

- Model 3 or Area 3

Unlike Structure 1, Structure 2 lets you break down all the components of each model at the same time. For example, "Model 1" can also include the Data Collection, Experimental Design, Numerical Example, Results, and Discussion sections. Structure 2 helps you to close out one area before moving to the next; this may ensure that your Dissertation Committee members don't forget all that you have presented.

4. **Final Edits**

It is always a good idea to hire a Dissertation-focused copy editor and proofreader. They can correct your spelling,

punctuation, and grammatical errors, plus review and revise your formatting— making sure it is done correctly throughout your Dissertation document, and Presentation before you officially submit your document to your Advisor(s); and share your Presentation with your Dissertation Committee members a few days before Defense Day.

Download your graduate school's/institution's checklist(s) to make sure you have included everything that needs to be in your Dissertation document and Presentation. Send your final Dissertation document to your Advisor(s) for one more review. Most institutions have a session where they go through all the guidelines to complete the process to graduate. Make sure you attend—there are certain deadlines you cannot miss and ignorance is not an excuse.

5. **Practice**

Practice going through your Dissertation Defense Presentation with your Dissertation Chair as well as peers, who will give you constructive feedback. It helps if these peers are outside of your field— the questions they might ask you will let you know if your Presentation is clear or needs more work. As your Defense Day draws near, wind down your practice time because you don't want to overdo it. Create a script to help you stay focused.

6. **Additional Tips**

   a. Start working on your Dissertation documents and Dissertation Defense Presentation *__early__*.

   b. Get plenty of rest before your Final Defense Day.

   c. If you can, eat a good breakfast; it will be a long day. No matter the outcome, plan on treating yourself to a really good lunch.

   d. Remember, you are the expert about your research—speak confidently. Today, you will become a colleague.

   e. Enter/submit all of your final documents on time for graduation.

We surely cannot leave this chapter without affirmations. You are right on the verge of officially becoming a Doctor of Philosophy (Ph.D.)! What I like to tell people is that once you have made up your mind to attain a Ph.D., you are now just going through the process to make it official.

Congratulations, *Doctor*, you've successfully passed your Final Defense and just earned your Ph.D.! You are officially *PhinisheD*!!

As we prepare to close out this chapter and section, let's affirm the great milestones you've already completed, as you prepare to cross over your Phinishline.

I am Dr. _____!

I am making an impact with my research!

My Final Defense is successful!

I am an expert in _____!

What's inside of me is coming forth!

I can do hard things!

I am bringing awareness to _____ through my research!

I represent _____!

P.P. (Post Ph.D.)

"DONE IS BETTER THAN PERFECT."

— SHERYL SANDBERG[8]

8Master Academia. December 21, 2022. Top 10 Motivational quotes for Ph.D. Students. Retrieved from https://master-academia.com/phd-motivational-quotes/.

CHAPTER 8
Rediscovering Yourself

Congratulations! You have finally made it to your Phinishline and walked across the stage at graduation. Hopefully, the reality of your major accomplishment is starting to sink in— if it hasn't already. Yes, you really have finished! No more Dissertation writing, working on research, or checking in with your Advisor(s).

At long last, your Ph.D. degree journey is **complete**. Now, you suddenly have *a lot* more free time at your disposal (remember the focus of Chapter 5— Emotional Rollercoaster?). You don't have to skip any more (important) events; you can begin to get back to your life and create a new/revised daily routine. At least that's how it feels.

You may actually find yourself trying to put the pieces of your life back together. After spending so much time as a student— and identifying with work and overload— it may take some time for you (and those closest to you) to adjust.

After I crossed my Phinishline, I found it hard to rest. I had phantom Ph.D. feelings— like I'd just missed a deadline, or I needed to work on something. In those moments, I would remind myself that my Ph.D. journey was complete. I had to give myself a chance to rest. And ample time to fully enjoy my family. I needed to *rediscover* myself again— on the other side of my Ph.D. journey— now as a successful Ph.D. graduate.

As we started our journey through this book, I encouraged you to think about your desired ending to help you better develop your story and identify your "Why." Utilizing the positive strategies found in every chapter of this book serves as a form of identity theft protection. We are internally monitoring what is going into our minds— ensuring that we are valuing and nurturing the correct narratives about ourselves.

At this moment, I (once more) want you to go back and reread Chapter 1. Now, ask yourself those three (3) questions— in this way:

1. "Why _**did**_ I want to pursue a Ph.D.?"

2. "What _**did**_ I hope to achieve?"

3. "What steps _**got**_ me there?"

Reread your previously written answers to these three questions from when you were pursuing your Ph.D. and now answer them from this new perspective— as a graduate. Analyze how your answers are similar or different from before you received your Ph.D. versus now, adjusting to life after becoming a Doctor of Philosophy.

So, what did I do after crossing over my Phinishline? I spent the following months slowly reintroducing all the things I loved back into my life and daily routine(s); I also spent _**a lot**_ of time sleeping.

Additionally, I did my best to avoid all kinds of work— except for job hunting. I started applying and interviewing for various jobs; however, nothing seemed to be going through. I was getting discouraged trying to figure out my next steps—and determine where I was headed. (We will focus more on the job-hunting process in the next chapter.)

Now, let's identify some things you _**can**_ do during this time as well as some things to think about.

Take out at least one (1) blank sheet of paper and write down your responses to these thoughts. This can help shape your future trajectory— it deserves your intentional time and energy. Don't rush through it!

1. You may have forgotten what you like to do for fun and/or your favorite hobbies. **Now** is the perfect time to rediscover them and even find some new ones.

2. Give yourself time to find out what you want to pursue. I spent many days writing down what I was interested in, work-wise, and aligning these interests with my goals and values.

3. Give yourself space to pause and enjoy your freedom again.

4. Reflect on what you learned throughout your Ph.D. journey about yourself.

5. Reflect on even the _trauma_ you may have experienced throughout your Ph.D. journey— with your focus being on working through it and letting it go. You don't want any past hindrances distracting you in the next phase(s) of your life.

6. Be open to what you discover even if it's outside your comfort zone—nor what you expected.

7. **Write a letter to yourself, reminding you of who you are and what you bring to the table**. Read it every day until you believe it!

On the flip side of rediscovering yourself, is what I like to call _representation_. If you are a person of color, this is especially weighty. You may feel like the newest celebrity within your family. Whatever you decide to pursue next will result in you being the new kid on the block. In each of these instances, the way you show up is different. What you pour out for others is also different. Don't lose sight of what you have placed in certain spaces. Keeping all of these points in mind, let's affirm this new season.

I am more than my title of "Doctor."

I have permission to realign my goals and values with where I want to be _now_.

I have permission to pivot!

I deserve space to rediscover myself.

"ACT AS IF WHAT YOU DO MAKES A DIFFERENCE. IT DOES."

— WILLIAM JAMES[9]

9Master Academia. December 21, 2022. Top 10 Motivational quotes for Ph.D. Students Retrieved from https://master-academia.com/phd-motivational-quotes/.

CHAPTER 9
What Path(s) Should You Take?

During your *rediscovery* season, you might be trying to figure out what professional/career path(s) you should take. I often challenge graduate students to think about this **throughout** their Ph.D. journey. Having a general idea of what professional/career path(s) you want to take ensures you are doing what's necessary to proceed in the right direction(s).

There are many gurus, thought leaders, coaches, and experts who will try to tell you what you should or should not do. You must take time in your rediscovery season to know what you want and make plans to achieve your desired professional/career goals.

In general, there are roughly three (3) common professional areas that you can go into upon completion of your doctoral degree: Academia, Industry, and Entrepreneurship. Remember: you are planning **your** life— your new path(s) can include just about anything; keep an open mind and utilize your sharp research skills. You will be surprised at how your new season unfolds. Here is a snapshot of how to prepare for all three common professional areas.

Academia

Let's start with Academia. There are many paths you can take based on whether you choose a Tenure Track position or a Non-Tenure Track position. The positions can also vary, based on the type of institution you choose.

Tenure Track

Under Tenure Track, you will be evaluated based on your teaching, research, and service skills. You are also able to move through the ranks starting as an Assistant Professor, progressing to an Associate Professor, and then becoming a Full Professor. It is really good to have a strong research plan in place to hit the ground running.

Non-Tenure Track

Under the Non-Tenure Track, you can become a Lecturer, Adjunct Professor, Research Professor, Teaching Professor, or Professor of Practice. This is normally not a long-term position; plus, unless your title has the word "Research" in it, your main responsibility is to _**teach**_.

While employed as a Faculty Member, it is also possible to move into an Administrative position. I recommend that you wait until you have learned the department's culture— and have officially received Tenure at your chosen institution, before pursuing such a position. If you do decide to go down this path, you will need to prepare materials for your applications and the required interviews.

Applications

Most Academia-specific job applications are now completed entirely online. They will oftentimes require you to type in some (if not all) of the information that can be found on your Curriculum Vitae (C.V.) and/or Resume. I suggest having that document handy— or creating a specific Microsoft Word document with all of this information ready for you to copy and paste the applicable text while completing your applications in their respective online systems.

You will also need to identify three to four (3–4) people who are willing to be professional and personal references. I encourage you to ask if your chosen references would also be willing to write you letters of recommendation.

Letters of Recommendation

Letters of Recommendation are very important. You want to identify people who can positively speak to your abilities as a teacher and researcher, giving a broad overview of who you are to the hiring committee.

Your Three (3) Statements

In addition to providing References and Letters of Recommendation, your Academia applications will need to include three (3) different documents for the hiring committee to review: your Teaching, Research, and Diversity statements.

Teaching Statement

Your Teaching Statement should be one (1) page. It should describe your personal approach to teaching. You should list your different teaching experiences in various capacities and share examples of how you can run a classroom. You should also mention the different pedagogical methods you have used/will use to engage students. Lastly, you can also mention a little about the mentoring you do with students. The key is to give the hiring committee an overview of your teaching style(s) and share what they can expect to see from you in the classroom.

Research Statement

Your Research Statement can vary in length. However, be mindful of your reader(s)—remember that your application is more than likely one of *many* being considered. A succinct and targeted statement is always best. This statement should highlight your current research, extensions, future research, and potential funding sources. You want to show how your research is distinct from your Advisor's (or Advisors') research. Be sure to show a clear connection between you and your desired department and university's vision and/or goals.

Diversity Statement

Your Diversity Statement should include information on the diversity, equity, and inclusion (D.E.I.) initiatives you have participated in during your studies and/or professional career. The three (3) key areas you can highlight are how your D.E.I. initiatives are shown throughout your research, teaching, and service. This statement should also be one (1) page in length. Be sure not to embellish or fabricate your experience(s).

Interviews

Interviews can happen either in person or virtually via a videoconference platform.

Screening Interview for Academia

A Screening Interview happens after the hiring committee identifies a pool of applicable candidates— those they feel best match the qualifications listed on the job posting. From there, you will converse either by phone or via a video conference platform. The length of your interview could range from 30 to 60 minutes. If you successfully complete this portion of the hiring process, you may be invited to do an on-site interview. The on-site interview can take place either in person or virtually.

In-Person Interview for Academia

The In-person Interview process for Academia is normally one to two (1–2) days. Your host institution will let you know about the travel arrangements being made on your behalf. Make sure to ask any and all questions you might have while on campus. During your in-person interview, you might also be asked to have a **Talk** prepared.

The length of a Talk is normally one (1) hour—you should aim to talk for about 45 minutes, leaving approximately 15 minutes for questions and answers. A snippet from your Dissertation, along with future work, possible courses, and (potential) funding sources is a good outline for your Talk. Some institutions may also ask for you to prepare a mock teaching lesson presentation.

Please additionally note that you will have the chance to speak with various people while you're on campus throughout your stay.

Make sure to learn something about each member of the hiring committee to show that you did your homework. Finally, get rest beforehand, make sure to wear something comfortable, and be ready to talk about topics that are not related to or super-focused on Academia—especially during the lunch and dinner breaks. The last part of the interview normally involves going around with a realtor to see the city and scope out potential places to live.

Virtual Interview for Academia

The Virtual Interview process for Academia is quite similar to the In-person process; however, you will probably meet more people throughout the day, since you're online. Make sure you have a good lighting setup and test your internet connection the day before plus early on the day of your interview— to help decrease your chances of experiencing (any) technical difficulties. When you get a break, make sure to give your eyes a break and eat plus hydrate to ensure you have energy.

For both types of Academia-specific Interviews, make sure you are able to articulate why you believe you're a great fit for your desired department(s)'s open position(s). Make sure to do your homework, learning as much as you can about your desired university and department(s). Most importantly, when you're asked if you have any questions, your answer should be "Yes." I encourage you to have two to three (2–3) questions prepared for each person—even if some are the same questions. Remember: you're also interviewing (and reviewing) the institution from _your_ perspective. This place could be your home for a while; so, you want to make sure you are making a wise and educated choice.

After the interviews are over, the hiring committee's Deliberation period begins. You might even be asked to compose a Memo detailing what you would need before coming to the university— as well as add certain items to their standard startup package. I would start thinking about this as you learn more about the university. Once you are physically on the campus grounds, you can craft better what your Memo should look like for you.

Industry

If you do not want to go into Academia but love research, you can still pursue a career in Industry. In Industry, you typically work to provide solutions to problems in real-time. Whether it be a position within a company or a national lab, the key is to make sure you (once again) do your research.

Preparation

You should seek out information on rotational programs or programs that will allow you to experience multiple departments before settling on one. Many universities have information sessions where various companies will take time to review resumes and/or LinkedIn profiles, plus share other ways of connecting with these featured companies moving forward.

I encourage you to also join all of your Alumni Associations (especially for your undergraduate and graduate schools) as well as connect with any reputable Alumni that work with the companies you're researching. They can help you better navigate the companies' interviewing, hiring, and onboarding processes.

Another important form of preparation is reaching out to and connecting with recruiters on LinkedIn. They are often very willing to give you advice on how to prepare applications before submission and share preparation insights for the different types of interviews. There are also many people you can connect with, based on different interests, to also provide you with resources.

Most importantly, you need to make sure your Resume (and/or C.V.) shows how the skills you learned during your doctoral work translate to a specific job. Include keywords related to the various jobs you are applying for within the document. When writing out your tasks, make sure to also show your tangible achievements. If needed, seek out someone to help you write or review your written Resume (and/or C.V.) to better increase your chances of being contacted for an interview.

Interview for Industry

Before your interview (either in person, over the phone, or virtually), you should prepare a couple of answers to some of the most commonly asked questions. Here are a few of those questions and speaking prompts:

1. Tell me a little bit about yourself.

2. What is one of your strengths?

3. What is one of your weaknesses?

4. Be able to answer technical questions.

5. Be prepared to provide examples of meeting outcomes or using specific skills.

Your interview can either be one-on-one or with multiple people— even up to a whole team; be prepared to speak with a lot of people and discuss a wide range of topics. You should also make sure to review as much (public) information as possible about the company and the various programs plus resources provided for employees. Remember, you are also interviewing the company. You are trying to get a sense of the type of work and environment you are looking to join. Lastly, one to two (1–2) days after the interview, be sure to send a follow-up email thanking your interviewer(s) for their time. In the same email, you can make sure to ask (more) clarifying questions about the position's responsibilities and salary range, if needed.

Entrepreneurship

Some people choose to initially work in Academia or Industry and then transition into Entrepreneurship. I think this is a great idea. First, it gives people the opportunity to create new programs or initiatives that we have not yet seen. Second, it's another way for people to share their unique expertise on **_their_** terms.

The main key is to **_clearly determine what a (successful) entrepreneurial business looks like for you_**. Make sure your business showcases what makes you unique and the importance of how your created solutions successfully solve specific problems. Do your homework to determine the type(s) of business(es) you want to legally run and have a solid Business Plan. You can also work with a professional coach to help you organize the business side—which is also built-in support and accountability.

Some entrepreneurial businesses you can consider include:

1. **Public Speaking**

Make sure to create a Speaker deck that showcases your signature talks and/or topics. You will need to create a webpage and social media accounts that will allow people to connect with you— plus find out more about your speaking fees/rates and requirements.

2. **Coaching**

Determine the platform(s) you will use to house your videos and other information. Determine if you want to do one-on-one coaching, group coaching, or both.

3. **Non-Profit/For-Profit Business**

Find ways to create partnerships with other programs or organizations that might be helpful to leverage resources.

4. **Membership**

Provide consistent content to customers through an online platform and provide some in-person meet ups or programs. Here are some ways you can leverage access to your chosen community/communities.

5. **YouTube Channel**

Many people post free content on this platform to build up awareness about their business, plus brand, and establish their credibility in the field. Typically, after you reach a certain number of followers, you can begin to monetize your channel.

6. **Online Courses**

Creating free courses through Thinkific, Teachable, or Kajabi about a specific topic (or topics) helps others to learn more about your area(s) of expertise.

7. **Social Media**

All of your social media platforms can be utilized to share highlights into your day-to-day life plus information/updates about your entrepreneurial business(es). Social media also helps people get to know you personally and connect with you (and even create smaller groups of like-minded people) to get more targeted information.

8. **Webinars**

These can be used to help people learn (more) about various offers/promotions or programs you might have. They can even be used to build your email list and drive traffic to your business website and/or social media accounts.

Before we leave this chapter, let's affirm these great professional plans you are developing and the career choices you are making.

> **I am built for the journey of creating and planning a new path (or paths) for my career—now that I have my Ph.D.**
>
> **I am open to receiving what is meant for me.**
>
> **I am flexible.**

"WE MUST BE WILLING TO LET GO OF THE LIFE WE PLANNED
SO AS TO HAVE THE LIFE THAT IS WAITING FOR US."

— JOSEPH CAMPBELL[10]

10 Master Academia. December 21, 2022. Top 10 Motivational quotes for Ph.D. Students Retrieved from https://master-academia.com/phd-motivational-quotes/.

CHAPTER 10
Taking Care of Yourself

I remember it like yesterday: May 14, 2016, I graduated with my Ph.D. I was so grateful to see this day because I almost did not make it. **_Literally_**. A couple of weeks before graduation, I was not feeling so great— and I blacked out for a few seconds. My husband, who is thankfully very quick on his feet, laid me down on the floor (so the blood could flow back to my head) and then called 9-1-1. After they arrived, the paramedics said that was the perfect thing for him to have done at that moment. I was, then, taken to the hospital to go through a series of tests.

Apparently, I was so dehydrated it was hard to locate my veins. For the first time in my life, the lab technician had to draw my blood through the back of my hand. It seemed like I was waiting for forever to find out what was wrong. They told me I had a "Vasovagal response." I spent the next couple of days resting and taking it easy at home. It was clear that I needed to really take the time to pause and prioritize my health.

Why did I start off by sharing this story with you? I want this point to hit home: Your Ph.D. degree means absolutely nothing— especially if you are sick or dead or… fill in the blank: _____. All of my hard work would have been for nothing. If I had died, I would not have been able to fully celebrate or enjoy my major accomplishment.

Your Ph.D. journey can easily get you into a space where you feel like you must constantly produce something— anything. You feel like you can never take breaks; you need to always be working. You feel like everyone is graduating and progressing except for you. You get frustrated because you're not on the same page as your Advisor(s).

Please know that whether or not you take a break, your work will still be there tomorrow. The time you are now taking to rest and pour back into yourself is actually going to ***accelerate*** you.

To help you begin pouring back into yourself, I want you to write out your answers to these four (4) levels of commitment questions:

1. What can you commit to doing for yourself ***daily***?

2. What can you commit to doing for yourself ***weekly***?

3. What can you commit to doing for yourself ***monthly***?

4. What can you commit to doing for yourself ***yearly***?

I encourage you to do your best to honor (stick with) these four levels of commitment— for a whole year.

As a student, you can sometimes feel like you are not able to live your life, especially during your graduate degree journey. Please know that it is possible to have a life— you just have to be strategic and have the proper support in place.

You need to strategically include:

Making time to rest!

Taking walks!

Meditating and/or praying!

Saying your affirmations!

Having your quiet time!

Binge watching your favorite shows!

Doing activities you love!

Pampering yourself!

Spending time with your family!

Taking vacations!

Eating right!

Exercising!

Getting a therapist!

Sleeping and taking naps!

Getting your regular checkups with respect to your health!

Now, let's affirm how you are making sure to rest and take better care of you.

I am able to prioritize my health.

I can and will take time to rest.

I am pouring back into myself daily, weekly, monthly, and yearly.

"TO BE YOURSELF IN A WORLD THAT IS CONSTANTLY TRYING TO MAKE YOU SOMETHING ELSE IS THE GREATEST ACCOMPLISHMENT."

— RALPH WALDO EMERSON[11]

11 Master Academia. December 21, 2022. Top 10 Motivational quotes for Ph.D. Students Retrieved from https://master-academia.com/phd-motivational-quotes/.

CHAPTER 11
Paying It Forward

As we come to the end of our time together, I want to congratulate you on successfully crossing over your Phinishline. I hope adding me (through this book) to your Ph.D. journey provided you with new insights, helpful skills, effective strategies, and great tips that made your doctoral process less stressful and more motivating. I also hope you felt encouraged to happily continue on your Ph.D. journey, and joyfully got hooded at your graduation ceremony.

My heart's desire is to add value to every person and audience I have the honor to encounter. At a young age, my parents instilled in me the habit of paying it forward. That's exactly why I wrote this book.

Now that you have officially ***Phinished*** your doctoral journey, it's time for you to determine how you can ***pay it forward*** to support those yet to cross over their Phinishline.

For me, I will pay it forward by:

1. Pouring into future Ph.D.s by cultivating their love for research while they are undergraduate students.

2. Encouraging the next generation of Engineers.

3. Mentoring students, starting from elementary school all the way through college.

4. Helping students see their potential and reach their goals.

5. Giving back to my community.

6. Utilizing my gifts and expertise to leverage opportunities for others.

7. And much more.

In conclusion, I have two more tasks for you to complete. Take ample time to reflect, and then write out the ways you will pay it forward.　　Next, write down your lessons learned to pass on to another Ph.D. Candidate working through their doctoral process. I also encourage you to share this book as well as your words of wisdom.

Thank you!

I will pay it forward by doing the following:

Dear Future Doctor of Philosophy (Ph.D.),

_____

_____

_____

_____

_____

_____

_____

_____

_____

_____

_____

_____

_____

_____

_____

_____

_____

_____

_____

_____

_____

_____

Sincerely,

Dr. _____

Once again, I encourage you to share this book as well as your words of wisdom with another Ph.D. Candidate currently on their journey to their Phinishline.

I hope you have enjoyed *Affirming the Ph.D. Within: Motivation to Walk the Journey to the Phinishline.*

Thank you!

References

Brown, Brené. 2018. *Dare to Lead: Brave Work. Tough Conversations. Whole Hearts.* New York, Random House.

Dowler, Frieda. 2022. "Victory Through An Identity Crisis." Blog. *Victory Christian Church.* 4 May 2022. https://victorycc.life/mdwkmotivation/victory-through-an-identity-crisis.

Kabat-Zinn, Jon. 2013. *Full Catastrophe Living: Using the Wisdom of Your Body and Mind to Face Stress, Pain, and Illness.* New York, Bantam Books.

Master Academia. *Top 10 Motivational quotes for Ph.D. Students.* Accessed 21 Dec. 2022.

https://master-academia.com/phd-motivational-quotes/.

Nieuwhof, Carey. "CNLP 356: Dharius Daniels on Leading with Relational Intelligence, Leadership Learned the Hard Way, and the Keys to Great Communication." Produced by Carey Nieuwhof. *The Carey Nieuwhof Leadership Podcast.* July 20, 2020. Podcast. Audio. 1 hour 14 minutes. https://careynieuwhof.com/episode356/. [Accessed 31 Aug. 2023].

"perfectionism." *Dictionary.com;* Accessed 31 Aug. 2023.

https://www.dictionary.com/browse/perfectionism.

"validation." *Oxford Reference;* Accessed 31 Aug. 2023. https://www.oxfordreference.com/view/10.1093/oi/authority.20110803115107111.

"worth." *Merriam-Webster;* Accessed 31 Aug. 2023. https://www.merriam-webster.com/dictionary/worth.

About The Author

Jessye L. B. Talley, Ph.D. is a professor in the field of Industrial and Systems Engineering. Dr. Talley is the Co-founder of Sisters Scholars, an organization that provides support and coaching to Ph.D. students throughout their doctoral journey. Outside of helping doctoral students, she coaches new faculty or aspiring faculty members to navigate through Academia and gain Tenure. You can read Dr. Talley's blog, find out more about her work, and follow her on social media by visiting her website: www.jessyelbtalley.com.

www.ingramcontent.com/pod-product-compliance
Lightning Source LLC
Chambersburg PA
CBHW081004120626
46546CB00010B/3003